BLACK

ANTHOLOGY

THE

TRUTH

BLACK

ANTHOLOGY

THE

TRUTH

POEMS FROM A BLACK MANS

PERSPECTIVE

BY

LYNNOR LATHAM GRAHAM

ISBN: 1-58820-081-7

1stBooks - rev. 6/26/00

To My Momma and My Children

THE CALLING

If I were to tell a story

Where would I begin

The story of all stories

At the end of a pen

This stories on my mind

It concerns those,

Of the Black mankind.

Once upon a time,

A long, long, time ago,

At the time of 1993,

It was twenty years or so ago,

What happened to brothers caring,

I don't know,

There were children, not, unlike myself,

Happy go lucky children, whom took pride in self,

Playing marbles, touch football and all,

We didn't have computer games yet, still the same,

We became adults in the world game,

What happened to the innocence,

What happened to the trust,

What happened to the caring,

The love that we must,

All savour,

That love we must begin again,

The love that must be passed on,

Time and time again,

To keep us from becoming,

Becoming a dead end,

Extinct we do no one any good,

Brothers heed the calling,

The calling in your hood...

Lynnor Latham Graham

IT'S ALL ABOUT LOVE,

It's all about LOVE,

We're born the same way,

Out of making LOVE,

Sin most say,

However you may,

It's all about LOVE,

When the first steps are taken,

Parents filled with JOY,

"CHAMMO-BABY,CHAMMO BABY",

That's baby talk we talk,

To see that child smile,

All the while,

"GOD"BLESS MY CHILD",

It's all about LOVE,

Now to guide that child,

There's so much you want to give,

Show that child how to live,

Or how to survive,

Thrive,

Stay alive,

As you did as a kid,

"Child WATCH THE PITFALLS",

"LEARN TO WATCH ALL",

"LEARN TO KNOW",

"WHEN TO GO",

"TO JUST SAY NO",

It's all about LOVE,

A MAMA"S CRY,

The screams of a black people,

Whom can't seem to get along,

Scared to speak to each other,

"THIS IS SO WRONG",

It's all about LOVE,

And sometimes it's a curse,

To SEE all I SEE,

But it's a SPIRITUAL GIFT,

IT's ALL ABOUT LOVE,

A STRONG LOVE WITHIN ME,

For BLACK HUMANITY,

A GIFT SOME SAY,

I'll SEE something today,

As I do every day,

And when it touches me, I'll write it down,

On what ever's around, paper off the ground,

A Doublemint wrapper, a napkin,

To you my friend,

A message from my heart to your soul,

IT'S ALL ABOUT LOVE...

Lynnor Latham Graham

THE BLACK CHILDREN OF TODAY

I want you to understand, the black children of today,

They're living in a black world, a black way,

When we were brought up, the world was grey,

But, mostly in the white way,

We did not have, Essence, Y.S.B. or B.E.T.,

All we had was each other, you and me,

We didn't have knowledge of the system at hand,

There were so many things we didn't understand,

We've always been compassionate,

We've always been strong,

We've always known that we have been wronged,

Back then we had no uzis, jet planes and crack,

No, it's their way now, of holding us back,

For we own, no planes, no poppy fields, no airports, in fact,

We still own very little, yet, still remain intact,

Intact and together, in so many ways,

Despite the, to young ones, the White devil, they say,

Is it coincedence, that's what we called them,

Back in the day.

I want you to understand, the black children of today,

They understand so much, yet, so little,

In a black world, a black way,

Many are strong, many a stray,

Many are disrespectful, many polite in everyway,

Many have been pushed, many have been killed,

Many have been incarcerated, many more will,

As I said before,

Intact and together, in so many ways,

They understand so much, yet, so little,

The black children of today...

Lynnor Latham Graham

HOW MUCH HEART

HOW MUCH HEART,

We must have,

To be a BLACK PEOPLE today,

All of the obstacles,

In our path,

In our way,

HOW MUCH HEART,

We must have,

To be a BLACK MAN,

To withstand and understand,

This country is not EQUAL yet,

The past we cannot forget,

If you look hard enough,

The past is still staring us in the face,

So DON'T BE BLIND,

HOW MUCH HEART,

We must have,

To be a BLACK WOMAN,

To withstand and understand,

9

To encourage and not discourage,

The BLACK MAN,

To help him,

To make him feel like a man,

To sometimes HOLD HIS HAND,

To sometimes JUST BE THERE,

To once in a while,

WIPE AWAY A TEAR,

Although all men won't admit it,

We're GLAD BLACK WOMAN YOUR THERE,

HOW MUCH HEART,

We must have,

TO ENDURE RODNEY KING AND THINGS,

How much heart we must have,

To keep our faculties intact,

To move forward only to be shoved back,

How much heart we must have,

To be so STRONG,

To ENDURE THE ENDURED SO LONG,

How much heart we must have,

And HOW MUCH HEART WE WILL ALWAYS KEEP,

FOR IT IS HEART THAT WE GATHER,

IT IS HEART THAT WE REAP
HOW MUCH HEART...

Lynnor Latham Graham

03/17/96

TIME TO WAKE UP

To watch a deteriorating generation,

To know, the realization,

Of the majority of a nation,

A genocide situation,

Of God's dominionated creation,

Black on black crime for compensation,

Seems it takes blacks doing time for

    elation,

We must introduce some type of vocation,

Stop all the nullification,

Take advantage of education,

Youth should be our dedication,

Justice is not justification,

More like isolation,

It's our obligation,

To stop the systems violation,

Cease black homicidation,

Curb the perpetuation,

Of the "so called," operation,

Get into visualization,

Of the systemization,

For there's definitely a formation,

Sea of power's a quotation,

From a frightful book of revelation,

Time to wake up...

Lynnor Latham Graham

Show Me The Way

I want to write, but don't know what to say,

Give me some wisdom Lord, show me the way,

As I flow with my pen, there's a thought,

That's coming in,

And the thought is,

Ask and it Shall be given ....

                Amen ....

The subject of life, a versatile strife,

You can ask husband, you can ask wife,

These things must come to pass, things that many knew

So why so disgusted when we hear the late news,

Things will not get better, they will only get worse,

Mankind is truly, his own curse,

There's a lack of knowledge, so many don't know,

Our children are walking in the darkness,

We must help them see the light,

Walking around in hoodies, both day and night,

Blowing each other away, we know it's not right,

It's sad, young ones, plight,

But to let you know, if these things must go,

It is us as a people, the way, we must show,

For it is our children, it is our youth,

We as a people knew, it doesn't take a detective, or a sleuth,

It doesn't take a private eye for us to see why,

So many, so young, have to die,

I know this story it can get pretty deep,

Think of all the mama's tears, think of how they weep,

Love at all times, we must reap,

Praise the Lord our souls to keep,

In order for a generation to survive,

In order for a generation to strive,

Those of us less fortunate, we mustn't criticize

They have no light yet, in their eyes,

Let's help them to help themselves attain,

The knowledge of the light, must be gained

                    Amen ....

Courts don't want you to discipline your child,

Let them grow up disobedient, let them grow up wild,

To enlighten those who don't know,

Long ago Commandments you were told,

The wisdom of the Bible, a child you must scold,

The order of the light, we must behold,

Now so many sell their souls,

16

Because they just don't know,

Just don't understand

No one told them of the MASTER plan,

Well I am going to tell, how it was, how it is,

and will always be,

In the beginning was the WORD and the

WORD was with God

And the WORD was GOD (John I)

Amen ....

Think to yourself I AM THAT I AM,

Hopefully you can hear the power,

Hopefully you've heard, the entire message

of these five words,

Say them loudly and you will begin to understand,

That great gift that GOD gave every man,

You are, I AM THAT I AM,

Amen ....

Remember at the beginning,

I didn't know what to say,

I AM THAT I AM

Showed me the way ....

Lynnor Latham Graham

LIVING CONDITIONS OF FAITH

Living conditions of faith,

Maybe you can relate,

At times there's love,

At times there's hate,

"I know how to work my toilet"

"Even if you don't,"

Wait,

Something to elate,

And a different color man,

Told me he understands,

"Bugged," I know,

But, I believe,

Deep within me,

And outer,

"Peace"

A love and understanding,

A presence,

At all times,

The Divine,

"One,"

"Perfect One,"

19

"His Son,"

"Our Father,".

Yet, we do not alter,

Instead, we faulter,

Past the wayside,

I tried, and try,

My treasures in Heaven,

And blessed,

That must be,

What makes me strong,

Living conditions of faith,

"Spandex,"

Summer times in,

Yet, to glance that way,

Is a sin,

I try to turn,

The other cheek, that is,

"Lord knows,"

"I must work on that,"

It's amazing,

He's traveled the same roads,

Or paths that I did,

At one time, the Lord, Himself,

Was a kid,

Yet, pure of pures,

No matter what the trial,

Yeah, though I walk through,

"To know,"

Thou art with me,

Keeps me sane,

Living conditions of faith,

To remain,

To attain,

Reach, always,

I reach,

Not to preach,

But at times, It's hard not too,

I am, and I am not alone,

Living conditions of faith,

Graffiti where I live,

So much to my wife,

And children,

I want to give,

and family, friends,

Co-workers, and people I don't even

know,

So, maybe you can understand,

The love within a man,

To want us all,

To have it to share,

To care,

While so many young, die,

Brothers,

"Why"?

And you can't even tell me,

You see,

It's really not meant to understand,

And it's amazing God wanted it that way,

"The Book," says,

"Lean not unto thy own understanding,"

"But, Trust in the Lord,"

"And in all your ways acknowledge Him,"

At times, even I forget,

At times you regret,

Yet, the Name we call in distress,

"Jesus Christ,"

Right,

Living conditions of faith,

Praise God, acknowledge,

At all times,

He that hath an ear,

Let him hear,

"Wisdom,"

And there's so many

Whom don't understand,

The Plan,

Plight that we bring upon selves,

It's not all that hard,

Living conditions of faith,

Understand,

Every minute,

Every hour,

The Principalities,

The Powers,

And the weapons,

We need to fight them,

Love, Peace, and Wisdom,

Not AK's,

O.K.,

No Nines,

No forty fives,

Killing to survive,

Another brother to stay alive,

That's not the way,

It's the wrong direction,

A strive for perfection,

One man did it,

And His name is above all others,

The last one to cry,

But you must know,

Living conditions of faith,

Amen...

Lynnor Latham Graham

NIGGER!

A name that was derived,

That in order to survive,

We had to tolerate to stay alive,

But now it's a word we should not quotate,

Before you use the word try to relate,

To it's heritage, it's beginning,

Let's make it an end,

"NIGGER" doesn't even sound right, my friend,

Since when did nigger become such a trend,

Nigger this, nigger that,

My nigger ain't where it's at,

Nigger is a word, used back in the day,

That brothers didn't use not even to play,

Nigger a word I'm sick of,

A word that makes me sick,

A word derived and given to us by hicks,

The white man, the klan, understand,

And like fools trying to be cool,

"WE" still use it!

Nigger so frequently in use,

"BY OUR BLACK YOUTH",

25

Unpleasant to the ear,

"WE" shouldn't even want to hear,

NIGGER,

MY NIGGER THIS, MY NIGGER THAT,

MY NIGGER AIN'T WHERE IT'S AT!

"OUR FOREFATHERS WERE DEMORALIZED",

"OUR FOREFATHERS WERE WHIPPED AND
TIED",

"CALLED NIGGER AS THEY CRIED",

CRIED IN PAIN AND AGONY,

AT THE WORD NIGGER , YOU SEE,

MY NIGGER THIS, MY NIGGER THAT,

MY NIGGER AIN'T WHERE IT'S AT ....

LYNNOR LATHAM GRAHAM

01/06/94

TO THINK THE THOUGHT

A generation so lost,

A place in time,

FORGOT,

No feelings,

No regrets,

YEARS THEY HAVEN'T SEEN YET,

So many things we did forget,

Or maybe we do know,

To think the thought,

But YOUNG BROTHERS,

DON'T THINK!

Killing EACH OTHER with ease,

Without realization,

Of GENOCIDATION!

GOD'S FIRST CREATION!

They can't see the CONSOLIDATION,

Of a BLACK NATION!

And it's SAD,

TO THINK THE THOUGHT,

Or maybe not,

Because it's scary,

BROTHERS SO LEERY,

OF THEIR OWN KIND,

NO PEACE OF MIND,

You tell them so,

They just figure,

YOU JUST DON'T KNOW!

"TIMES ARE DIFFERENT",

They say,

YOU DON'T UNDERSTAND,

ANYWAY,

OUR PLIGHT TODAY,

"YEAH O.K.

THE STREETS WILL ALWAYS BE

"THE STREETS",

OR THE NOW CALLED "SET",

AT ONE TIME "WE" OWNED THEM!

LEST WE FORGET,

TO THINK THE THOUGHT,

BROTHERS DYING SO YOUNG FOR NAUGHT,

IT'S KILLING OUR FUTURE,

AND YOUNG BROTHERS CAN'T SEE,

BLINDED BY THERE OWN STUPIDITY!

AN ENTIRE GENERATION,

OVERCROWDED PENALIZATION,

LET'S NOT FORGET INCARCERATION,

LET'S NOT FORGET GRAVEYARDS,

BROTHERS, SLOWLY OUTGROWING,

THE "SO-CALLED" MAJORITY,

BROTHERS KILLING BROTHERS WITH THE HELP

OF "AUTHORITY"!

LYNNOR LATHAM GRAHAM

02/12/95

A WRITING MOOD

A writing mood,

Something to brood,

To help those of us see,

Destination, tragedy,

To see, surely not, just me,

More and more taken away,

Day to day, new laws, new ways,

Cameras, lenses, recorders,

The size of quarters,

Privacy, no longer be,

Just you and me,

We're all watched,

More and more, you see,

There's a book of prophecy,

The last days, how it will be,

You'd think we'd try to alter,

But, instead we still faulter,

To the wayside, trying to hide,

So many have tried, to reason,

A new season, that is dawning,

Yawning, as if asleep,

So many poor, so many weep,

So many praise their souls to keep,

When you have a baby in your hands,

Then you can weep,

Weep for that baby, man,

For all that baby will endure,

There is no cure,

We all have to live our lives,

To the fullest,

So many push to die,

So many gave up the try,

So many whom haven't lived,

Die,

Not knowing what they had to give,

Now, they do not live,

At least six feet deep,

That hole looks to me,

Worms and doodle bugs creep,

To seep,

Through to you,

A hard head and your thru,

Not to chastise as I cry,

But, why so many children,

Why so many die?

Too late to start over,

The prophecies been told,

At least two thousand years old,

Things will only get worse,

Mankind truly his own curse,

So many don't understand;

And kids still think they know it all,

Life's not a movie,

You don't always come back,

Next episode,

A dead end mode,

Not to scold,

But I do hope this sticks in,

A sad sad story to begin,

From mother's womb to sure "nuf' doom,

Sadness and gloom,

Surrounding,

Siren sounding,

Heads pounding, to the pavement,

Stomped into cement,

Stabbings, shootings,

A snow storm, and looting,

Animals are animals,

Yet, we're civilized,

I realized,

A play on words,

But, not funny at all,

This play, any way,

Where's the love?

The understanding, and caring,

Of years ago,

Time's not moving slow,

Faster and faster it seems to go,

But at least it's not standing still,

Baby girls,

close your legs and keep them that way,

At least until your wedding day,

Baby brothers,

Go to school,

Quit holding your pants and being cool,

Children be children as long as you can,

Grown ups,

Learn to love your fellow man,

A message I hope you'll take heed,

For love is definitely in dire need,

Of love today,

That's all I'll say,

Not meaning to be rude,

A writin mood...

Lynnor Latham Graham

TIMES ARE A CHANGIN

We did things like dive over cars,
Moving, on a dare, for a cause,
Guys today, shoot at each other,
Times are a changin.

The people next door to us cared,
We were like family,
Times are a changin.

We used to walk down the street,
Not guarded, when we meet,
We used to say, what's happenin,
How you feel, have a nice day,
Times are a changin.

Today, yo my nigger, yo my boy,
My homey, and my dog,
Times are a changin.

Ringing doorbells, and runnin,

That was funnin no gunnin,
Times are a changin.

Happy to hold hands, get a smooch,
Or a kiss, maybe a little grinding,
Times are a changin.

A family at one time,
Was a man, and woman a child or two
Times are a changin.

Kids, teens and adolescents,
Respected their parents and elders,
On the bus, in the street, on the trains,
Times are a changin.

We used to cherish life,
And all of its gifts, and gave
Glory to Jesus Christ,
Times are a changin.

Brother has turned against brother,
Father against son,

Times are a changin.

Lynnor Latham Graham

LIFE (THE QUESTION)

Who can explain?

The joys, the pleasure, the pain,

Why is there sunshine?

Why is there rain,

How come laughter

Can mean your happy, or sad?

How comes there's good times?

And then there's bad,

Why are there, the rich,

And so many barely living,

Why is it to other countries,

We are giving?

Rather than taking care of those,

At home, whom are oppressed,

Depressed, and feel so all alone,

Why aren't the elderly respected?

Why so many children neglected?

Is that Life, or is It?

Lynnor Latham Graham

CRACK BABIES

Crack baby, crack baby, cause of what momma did,

I've seen kids on crack, cracked on kids,--

Born innocent, yet, already somewhat impaired,

Entering a world, already, with a care,

The lighting of a glassine pipe,

A generation, surely it will wipe,

By a mother with baby in womb,

Crack baby, crack baby,

Born, yet, doomed,

Doomed to a life of not understanding,

Not understanding doom, to it's life,

Cannot function in school, cannot read or write,

Crack baby, crack baby, with all of your might,

Entered into darkness, before you've seen the light,

Hopefully, you'll remember before you forget

And light a match, to your very first hit,

For that first hit won't be your last,

It will only lead-to your next, and final blast.

Crack babies, crack babies

Robbed, murdered, and stole,

Long before birth, your soul was sold,

Sold to a life of doom and misery,

Crack baby, crack baby,

Blinded before you could ever see.

Lynnor Latham Graham

A VOICE IN THIS WORLD

I am a voice in this world,
And I will be heard,
Heard through these pages,
Heard through the rages,
Of my sisters and brothers,
Heard and understood by others,

I am a voice in this world,
And I'm tired of reading about,
Little gang bangers being banged,
At one time we were hanged,
And it wasn't the same gang.

I am a voice in this world,
And I am infuriated,
By the homeless cries,
By crackheads, whom let babies die.

I am a voice in this world
And I'm tired of brothers,
Killing brothers.

I am a voice in this world
And I'm tired of parents,
Burying young children.

I am a voice in this world,
And I can't afford,
Change for everyone.

I am a voice in this world,
And the time has come,
For people to start caring
It must be done.

I am a voice in this world.

Lynnor Latham Graham

The Children I See

The children I see

Are in dire need

Of someone like me

Kidnappers, rapist, and killers

Labeled, should not, they be,

Sent away to an adult penitentiary,

The Children I see

May have shortened someones life expectancy

It's a childhood mistake of today

These are times, these are the ways,

These days,

The children I see

In Juvenile detention facilities,

Know of their seconds of stupidity,

It's amazing how they accept,

What they feel is-their responsibility

Awaiting their adult time

Aware and regret their crime

How do you explain

How can we get them to see
You cannot prepare, for a penitentiary,

The children I see,
Cry all the time,
Not for me to see,
But I do, and I feel,
For I know what's real,
Some of them, I'm sure, will make it,
Others, I don't know,
Some most definitely won't
Some have told me so,

The children I see
Are in dire need,
Of someone to talk to,
Someone to be,
Someone whom has a heart
Should see, I hope you'll agree,
These are my thoughts,
On the children that be,
Yes, just children, they be,
With all of my love,

And God bless thee,

God bless,

The children I see.

Lynnor Latham Graham

BROTHER TO SISTER

Smile, black sister,

For you are my strength,

Smile, black sister

For your time is well spent,

Smile, black sister

For, I've seen the work you do,

Smile black sister

For, I've seen you, bag and child in hand.

Smile black sister,

For appreciated you are,

And we must make you understand,

Smile black sister,

A smile from a black man...

Lynnor Latham Graham

THE BLACK STRUGGLE

You see it, and then you don't

You try to Ignore it, please, don't

Your will to won't, won't stop, if you don't,

Pay attention, take heed,

Help those helpable, too succeed,

We are in dire need

So, I've heard people say,

Dire need of someone to lead the way

Suppose the leaders are gone, gone to stay,

What do we do then?

We must learn our own way,

Yesterday, tomorrow and today,

We don't really need leaders,

To lead the way,

There's a lot of knowledge

In the youth today,

Unfortunately we're using it,

The wrong way,

Please, let us pray.

Lynnor Latham Graham

CONTEMPLATE

A young generation,

So full of hate,

Trying to elate,

Get youths to relate,

I've seen so many,

Seal their fate,

Trying to reach them,

Before it's too late,

They glamorize "Nines,"

They "dis" thirty-eight's,

Now's the time,

To realize,

No time to wait,

For time stands still,

For no man,

Because that's what you must be,

Teenage years in a Penitentiary,

Ma Ma can't get you out,

This time,

(One-eight-seven) The crime,

Not the one they gave me,

Wish God could save me,

And "He" may,

But not today,

Cuffs and chains,

Wrist ankles and waist,

Ten seconds of haste,

A lifetime of bells,

A different kind of hell,

No one to hear me yell,

Or maybe they don't care,

Yeah,

Contemplate,

Had to pull the trigger,

Cause I pulled the gun,

No time to hesitate,

No time to run,

All done,

I'm the one,

No need for tears,

Fifteen to twenty years,

To elate,

To relate,

To contemplate...

Lynnor Latham Graham

TIME

Blame it on time,

No one else to blame,

Not understanding things,

That happen in this crazy game,

Called life,

The strife,

The road that's traveled,

The decisions that are made,

Looking to change,

Rearrange,

Time,

Can't do it,

Blame it on time, Deterioration,

Of the free-est Nation,

Supposedly in the world,

An American,

Sure you can,

Do as you please,

With ease,

Just don't get caught,

Or you could rot,

Away,

Life and a day,

Time.

Blame it on time,

And is it worth it,

Facts,

No alibi's,

You didn't have to do it,

Just match the description,

Which so many of us do,

How true,

Crude,

And your not supposed to be rude,

"Thank you" your Honor,

And you too,

My faithful court appointed,

For the plea bargain,

That you anointed,

Sure I understand,

Three to five,

Or ten to twenty,

"Thank you" your Honor,

"That's plenty,"

of,

Time...

Lynnor Latham Graham

EVERY MAN SHOULD KNOW

Every man should know,

What it's like to have,

A woman by your side,

A woman that's yours, truly,

A bride,

A wife, a family,

Children, two or three,

Every man should know,

How it feels at the end of a day,

To step into your home,

And hear your children say,

"Yeah daddy's home,"

Every man should know,

To hear your wife every day,

Say "I love you,"

"I love you too,"

Every man should know,

How it feels to work and provide,

To kiss your babies boo boos,

As she cries,

Every man should know,

How it feels to look at your family,

Your home,

And know, you'll never be alone,

Every man should know,

What it's like to have your children think,

There's nothing daddy can't do,

Every man should know,

What it's like to provide,

That feeling deep down inside,

Where you know there's nothing,

At all you wouldn't do for your boys and

girls,

Every man should know,

What it's like to be a decision maker,

A giver not a taker,

To work for everything you own,

To lock the doors to your home,

Before you doze off to sleep,

Praise the Lord your souls to keep,

Kiss the wife and children,

Good night,

Sleep tight,

Don't let the bed bugs bite,

Every man should know...

Lynnor Latham Graham

GENERATIONS

Great, Great, Great, Great, Grandma,
Stolen on a ship,
Great, Great, Great, Great, Grandma,
Taken on a long trip.

Great, Great, Great, Grandma,
Born of here, but her heart is still across the water,
Great, Great, Great, Grandma,
Gives much love to her sons and daughters.

Great, Great, Grandma,
Working cotton and tobacco fields,
Great, Great, Grandma,
Rubbed up by the master,
Whenever He feels,

Great Grandma
Carrying on the stories of old.
Great Grandma
Oh, what stories, glorious stories,
She told.

Grandma, we've come, too long a way,

For us not to speak, for us not to say,

Grandma,

For us to be this way,

It's hard not to say

Drugs and guns are putting us away.

MA MA,

Let us Pray.

Lynnor Latham Graham

DON'T JUDGE ME AT FIRST SIGHT

Don't judge me wrong or right,

For if you do, you might,

Not get it right,

I'm nobody's stereotype,

One day I may,

Wear a suit and tie,

Why?

Because I feel that way,

A lot of times, I'm quiet,

And have nothing to say,

A stupid comment,

And that way I'll stay,

Ain't got much to say, today,

Don't judge me at first sight,

Don't judge me wrong or right,

For if you do, you might,

Not get it right,

I'm not always quiet,

Sometimes I have a lot to say,

Over eighty people, including children,

Dead,

Over four-hundred hurt,

One somebody's spurt,

Of anger,

Of hate,

To relate or better yet elate,

The pity,

That Wednesday in Oklahoma City,

But death happens every day,

Man kills wife,

Children blow each other away,

And we're civilized,

Just want peace,

Peace of mind,

Peace to all mankind,

Even those on the other side of the world,

Whom I don't even know,

peace to the man in the street,

Walks with his cup like a police on his beat,

I don't have change for everyone,

Yet,

I give,

To live,

I'm just that way,

So don't you even say,

I'm this or that way,

Don't judge me at first sight,

Don't judge me wrong or right,

For if you do, you might,

"Not" get it right,

I'm nobody's stereotype,

Today and tomorrow,

Is definitely not the same,

Different way of doing things,

A different approach I bring,

Hypothetically speaking,

Supposing,

An Adam and Eve theory,

To queery,

The thought,

No plot,

But if all were made,

From the only two on Earth to get laid,

The ultimate "Mom and Dad,"

Unless you and me have been had,

Always told it was bad,

The right way's a man and a woman,

A boy and a girl,

That to me means,

We're all brothers and sisters,

You see?

Together we could wipe out poverty,

Stop wars and save the waters,

Teach love to our sons and daughters,

We must fix where we faulter,

Try to alter,

And not repeat the past,

Living is supposed to last,

Parents are not supposed to bury their

young,

There should be no juries to be hung,

No sad songs to be sung,

We should be in harmony,

You should see all that I see,

Or stop ignoring it,

This is how the thoughts creep,

Writing's a blessing I reap,

My thoughts can be deep,

I praise the "Lord" my soul to keep,

To think as I weep,

That doesn't scare the children any more,

I deplore,

Implore,

As did Malcolm

As did Martin,

And over two-thousand years ago,

"Jesus" said so,

Let there be peace,

And now you should know,

Don't judge me from first sight,

Don't judge me wrong or right,

Don't judge me without,

Judge from within,

Peace and much love,

To all my kin...

Lynnor Latham Graham

AN EVERY DAY OCCURRENCE

An every day occurrence
Shouldn't be a black childs life,

An every day occurrence,
shouldn't be, man killing wife,

An every day occurrence,
Shouldn't be, homeless in the street,

An every day occurrence
Shouldn't be, on guard, when we meet,

An every day occurrence
Bullets fly,
Women die,
People, with no where to go,

An every day occurrence,
Shouldn't be so...

Lynnor Latham Graham

I WRITE

I write and at times,

Not knowing where to begin,

I have no idea where it will end,

Yet,

I try to relate to you,

A message from my heart to you,

At the beginning of time,

Who can really say what happened,

They weren't there,

But,

To care,

The word "Nigger,"

Used at a flare,

Brothers don't dare,

To realize,

This word derived,

From us being deprived,

Of ourselves,

Yet,

They used it,

I write,

And I see a lot of hate,

In young brothers,

A lot of hate indeed,

Let's say one thousand brothers,

Lived on a city block,

Give one half of them tech-nines,

The other half,

Glochs,

Think of the ratio,

These numbers are low,

Seems so grim,

A future that's dim,

If he don't get me,

I'll get him,

Now tell me,

Is it us, or is it them?

Everybody saying "recognize,"

"It all ain't good,"

But maybe somebody will listen,

Although all of you should,

I've been your age,

And you've never been mine,

But,

Time waits for no man,

Understand,

A plot for you not to make it,

When in fact you can,

Nobody said it was easy,

And I won't tell you a lie,

But nothing beats a failure,

But a try,

Long life and serenity,

Should be a destiny,

TO foresee,

Us to be,

Daisies,

Underground at sixteen,

That's what I mean,

Being played to the utmost,

Yet,

We boast,

Of a young brother lying in the street,

To meet his "so-called" destiny,

I write,

And you don't know what this does to me,

It hurts to see,

A man that worked all his life,

And he's homeless,

That doesn't make sense to me,

In America to be this way,

"land of the free,"

The things I see,

And feel,

The sad thing is it's real,

Yet,

There's always tomorrow,

Time borrowed,

For your tomorrow's,

Soon become yesterdays,

And the good ole days,

I guess what I'm trying to say,

Is think of what you want today,

A goal,

A plan of your own,

To stay in school,

Knowledge must be known,

It won't be long,

Before you're grown,

And hopefully ready for life,

We've all had to struggle,

We've all had our strife,

but that is what makes this,

Thing we call life,

Don't take it for granted,

That greatest gift of all,

No time to ponder,

No time to stall,

To all of yau'll,

I write...

Lynnor Latham Graham

PEOPLE

People, dying

People, trying to make a way,

People, learning more to hate each and everyway,

People, living together, but yet, so far apart

People, live next door, but I don't know who they are.

You got a man in the street,

He's robbed and he's beaten,

The shoes are taken off of his feet.

You got children everywhere who don't really care.

Because, they ain't got enough to eat.

People, I guess you've noticed, there is so little love

People what In the world are we thinking of?

People we all must learn to really care,

People help a fellow man learn to share.

People, I ask of you, tell me, what are we gonna do

People, I'll give a try to help, but you must help me too.

People, we all have got to lend that helping hand,

People, It's time right now, we all must take a stand,

People...

Lynnor Latham Graham

HOW COME I CAN SEE?

How come I can see,

Poverty,

Young brothers astray,

Black lives all array,

How come I can see,

How come I can say,

We're doing ourselves in today,

How come I can see,

Drugs on every other comer,

Sisters hoing,

Sisters on the stroll,

Playing a role,

A hit of crack,

They're on their backs,

Or putting things in their mouths,

A certain part of anatomy,

World' oldest profession,

Discretion,

Transgression,

How come I can see,

Brothers killing at will,

Societies ill will,

Police, judges, penitentiaries,

If not shot and killed,

Shoot another and still,

A young black life,

Wasted,

I've tasted,

The system,

And found it to be distasteful,

Disgraceful,

Not justified,

There is no justice inside,

There is little justice outside,

But at least,

You can live,

You can have a woman,

You can have a job,

You can have some freedom

You can never be equal,

That's another sequel,

That may be entirely,

Another life,

How come I can see...

Lynnor Latham Graham

SO MANY JUST DON'T KNOW

To watch,

To know,

It hurts us so,

So many just don't know,

Can't comprehend,

It's not a beginning,

It's a dead end,

One gun two brothers done,

One buried,

One's boxed in,

One's penalized,

My friend,

Lost the "so called" freedom

Freedom for life,

No children,

No goals,

No wife,

Inside looking out,

The wrong kind of clout,

Brothers must realize,

Open our eyes,

It's easier to get locked up,

Than it is to stay out,

Without a doubt,

To watch, to know,

Told you so,

So many just don't know...

Lynnor Latham Graham

A RAINDROP HIT THE GROUND

If you've never heard the sound,

Of a raindrop hit the ground,

A tingly soft pound,

Or it can be hard,

The sound,

If you've never heard the sound,

Of birds flocking to the ground,

The flutter of their wings all around,

It's a whipping, whirling, whomp,

The sound,

If you've never heard the sound,

Of mornings silent light,

Creeping from day to night,

If you've never heard these sights,

It's not right,

This plight,

It's rather profound,

Nine millimeter shells,

Hitting the ground,

Children falling down,

Some people this astounds,

Now I know,

And I understand,

When my heart pounds,

And I'm so content,

At peace,

At the sound I found,

If you've never heard the sound,

Of a raindrop hit the ground...

Lynnor Latham Graham

PLEA BARGAIN

Plea bargain, for lesser time,

Plea bargain, for an uncommitted crime,

Plea bargain, for something you didn't do,

Plea bargain, locked up, case is thru,

Plea bargaining,

I thought they wanted truth,

Innocent until proven guilty,

Please,

I think not,

I think it's backwards,

Because no one I know,

Gets arrested, innocently, so,

Guilty until proven innocent,

Jury by your peers,

I've never seen any of them,

In my neighborhood,

Jury trial will get you ten to twenty,

Plea bargain four to eight,

Not to logical to wait,

Plea bargain for lesser time,

Plea bargain for an uncommitted crime.

Lynnor Latham Graham

A GIFTED POET

A Gifted Poet,

Knows it,

When they don't know,

What they're going to say,

And it comes out anyway,

Because he has a heart,

He knows from the start,

Or better yet,

Feels with such compassion,

That at times he rations,

And he knows he's holding back,

For the feelings,

Will at times make you cry,

A scene when Old Yeller dies,

A scene when Whoopi tries.

To be so strong,

So long the agony,

The pain,

One endures in life,

The Color Purple,

The title,

An example to be trampled,

And still remain,

Sane.

A Gifted Poet,

Knows it,

Although,

He doesn't know the outcome,

At times the damage is done,

To be falsely accused,

To feel used,

Not to be trusted,

Disgusted,

To a point,

Where you no longer care,

You'll find someone else,

If you dare,

Because according to them,

You've already been there,

The trust is gone,

And you want to take a trip by yourself,

The signs,

An analytical mind,

So hard at times,

You may hurt me,

But you'll never know,

I refuse to let it show,

Maybe it's time we let go,

The trust is gone,

And I don't think it will ever come back,

Time to find what we lack,

Even if it is someone else.

A Gifted Poet,

Knows it,

And at all times,

What's written is done,

Not always fun,

Because you see,

More than others do,

You feel so deep,

So true,

You see things at times that destroy you,

As a little kid,

Snatches an old lady's pocketbook,

And kicks her with his feet,

Drags the old lady on the concrete,

Because she won't let go,

But, you need a fix,

And she doesn't know,

She's holding on to everything,

She's got,

And it's not a lot,

It's vital,

This plot.

A Gifted Poet,

Knows it,

Although at times it seems asinine,

To know and believe,

A divine,

A divine one does exist,

A realist,

For sure,

But a feeling of God,

with you at all times, Is mine,

And It's what keeps me sane,

To know that I am blessed,

And so are you,

If you take time to realize,

The prize,

The Gift,

That's within you,

We are all special,

In our own way,

There's only one you,

It's true,

So live,

The best you can,

Realize a man is a man,

He has a purpose,

Whether he realizes it or not,

Life's the most precious thing we've got,

A Gifted Poet,

Knows it....

Lynnor Latham Graham

EXPLAINING BLACK TO WHITE

To take on the task,

Thinking as I write,

EXPLAINING BLACK TO WHITE,

First of all,

There's the pigment,

Not a figment of the imagination,

This nation,

Judges from without,

Definitely not from within,

But the color of the skin,

So when you tell me,

"We're just like you",

That's thru,

That's dead,

WRONG,

So untrue,

At birth there's strikes,

You're born with one,

We're born with two,

"POOR AND BLACK",

Poor meaning monetarily,

Black (IN THIS COUNTRY) meaning unfortunately,

Two strikes against you,

And the way I see it,

"YOU" meaning white,

Get to earn yours as you go,

You're not born an outcast,

Future's been made in the past,

"That's just the way it is",

You've heard the phrase,

"I EXPERIENCE IT",

"That's just the way it is",

Step on the elevator,

And for some reason,

"You grab your bag a little tighter",

And give me that fake grin,

A purse,

Not a curse,

"That's just the way it is",

"Heads I win",

"Tails you lose",

"A different set of rules",

"And if you don't get it",

"That's not my problem",

"From way back when",

"Grandma's roof was tin",

Like so many promises made,

Fade Fade Fade,

Fade to black,

A sequel to be equal,

EXPLAINING BLACK TO WHITE

EXPLAINING BLACK TO WHITE,

Most say it can't be done,

Imagine on the run,

A teenage youth toting a gun,

Not always because you want to,

Not just for fun,

Running to keep from being locked,

Gunning to keep from being Gloched,

Blunted because of the things that are seen,

Can you imagine POVERTY,

Estimated by a so-called SOCIETY,

Babies having babies,

To get PAID,

Get laid,

To have something coming in,

Every other week,

The peak,

Of things most won't comprehend,

To be known from the outside,

Not from within,

After a drink or two,

"Oh yeah",

"I have a black friend too",

The things you do,

And what's AMAZING is "YOU" can't see it",

RODNEY KING BEAT DOWN ON VIDEO,

YET "YOU DON'T SEE IT",

"YOU" were given a front lawn to play in,

I on the other hand,

Had the streets,

Dark dilapidated hallways,

Seems we were always,

Talking of a better day,

"HERE'S SOMETHING ELSE TO PONDER",

"WE CAN'T HAVE THE BLACK PANTHERS",

"BUT YOU KLAN",

Fit the description and you can,

Alter your plans,

"IT WAS A BLACK MAN",

"FIVE FOOT TEN",

"WEARING A BASEBALL CAP",

"THAT'S A WRAP",

A trap that never ceases to fail,

To bitch and wail,

To plea bargain for just a LITTLE TIME,

"A SALE FROM ETERNITY",

"PEERS" just like you and me,

"ALTHOUGH I'VE NEVER SEEN ANY OF THEM IN

MY HOOD",

"I GUESS THAT'S GOOD",

THREE TO FIVE,

EXPLAINING BLACK TO WHITE

Rather than seven to ten,

To lose a little to win,

Bargaining time,

Even if you didn't commit the crime,

Their word against mine,

And then the negativity of my heritage,

Because I'm black I lack,

And to imagine it's set up that way,

BLACK-TAIL,

BLACK-LIST,

BLACK-BALLS,

BLACK-FISTS POUND THE GROUND,

All around the sounds sound,

Equality still unfound,

Profound you must think this sounds,

We all can't be wrong,

We all can't be having the same nightmare,

We have to survive in your world,

You could never survive in mine,

Even if you've lived there,

Even if you think you care,

109

It doesn't matter,

No nonsense,

A BLACK EXPERIENCE,

And you must be BLACK to experience it,

I'M TRYING REAL HARD TO BE SIMPLISTIC,

But most of all REALISTIC,

A plight that's never been right,

EXPLAINING BLACK TO WHITE...

Lynnor Latham Graham 03/24/96

BLACK SO BLACK

Born into a world,

That steps on your dreams,

Black so black,

So it seems

Everything' not,

Peaches and cream,

Black so black,

So it seems,

We've all been there,

Those of us whom do understand,

Black so black,

All over this land,

Keep your head up,

PLEASE,

Keep your pride,

I see so many,

Lost causes,

I CRIED,

I TRIED,

AND TRY,

AND TRY AGAIN,

Black so black,

The talent,

THE STRENTGH,

The time spent,

Trying to live legit,

SOMETIMES,

I WANT TO QUIT,

JUST LET GO,

BUT I CAN'T,

BECAUSE I KNOW,

AND TELL OTHERS SO,

BE STRONG!

BE TRUE!

BE ONLY YOU!

STRIVE!

THRIVE!

DRIVE!

SURVIVE!

BLACK SO BLACK!

TO STAY ALIVE!

YOU KEEP GETTING REEMED!

BLACK SO BLACK!

SO IT SEEMS...

LYNNOR LATHAM GRAHAM

02/12/96

ROACHES

Roaches, roaches, on the crawl,

Roaches, roaches, in the hall,

Roaches, roaches, where I live,

Roaches, roaches, plenty to give,

Roaches, roaches, I've complained,

Roaches, roaches, drive some insane

Roaches, roaches, all my life,

Roaches, roaches, struggles and strifes,

Roaches, roaches, struggles are hard,

Roaches, roaches, stuck in lard,

Roaches, roaches, roaches in fact

Roaches, roaches, spray them, they come back,

Roaches, roaches, in the sink,

Roaches, roaches, just don't think,

Roaches, roaches, where you at?

Roaches, roaches, SPLAT

Lynnor Latham Graham

NEVER ANOTHER YOU

Never another you, my brother,

Never another your point of view,

Never another you, my brother,

Understand,

Billion of people across this land,

Africa, London, Thailand,

Places you can only begin to comprehend,

But, "Check it,"

Never another you, my brother,

Never another,

"Tomorrow I'm gonna do this,"

Age seventeen,

No hopes, no dreams,

By any means, it is deemed,

Insanity, it seems,

Chillin, illin with my crew,

That little voice said not to,

But, I ain't goin' out like dat,

Shots fired into the crowd,

Rat-tat-tat-tat, that was that,

My boy got bucked,

My boy got dead,

A too common view,

Little brothers killing little brothers,

Never another you, my brother,

Never another, "what I ain't gonna do,"

"Cause It won't happen to me,"

Well, let's say it did,

Seventeen in jail,

Life your bid,

For something you did as a kid,

Speaking of kids, "you can't have any,"

Now your name can't be carried on,

The next generation is gone,

Your homey, the one shot and died,

Can't be carried on,

Another generation long gone,

"Now, do you understand?"

An outcry throughout this land,

Why parents, at home they want you to
     stay,

And they pray, you don't get blown away,

When your out, that you may be home,

Not out on the corners,

Not chillin with your crew,

Not doing the things, you do,

Take away you,

And no one knows the capacity,

Of what might've been,

In the long run,

At this speed we ride,

If we don't realize, Genocide,

There will be no future,

The movie 2001 Odyssey,

No one in this movie,

Looks like you or me,

You see.

Never another you, my brother,

Never another you,

Think of all the things you didn't do,

All the places you've never been to,

In the entire planet,

There's never another you,

My brother,

Never another you...

Lynnor Latham Graham

YOUNG BROTHERS SEE

My mind's workin hard,
Trying to stay involved,
Trying to help the young brothers see,
They don't listen to me.

The young brothers today
Have no respect for anyone, anyway,
Gotta make that doe in a fast way.

My mind's workin hard,
Trying to stay involved,
Trying to help the-young brothers see,
They won't listen to me.

Brothers locked up for centuries,
Held back or down for centuries,
Yet, there still building penitentiaries,
Young brothers, you must see,
You think we are free,
Brainwashed, we cannot be,
For we are not free.

Not free from welfare,

Not free from poverty,

Not free to be you,

Not free to be me,

Trying to help,

The young brother see.

Lynnor Latham Graham

I'M SORRY

I'm sorry, I'm angry,
About inflation and high tax,
I'm sorry, I'm angry
I'm angry, that's fact.
Trying to deceive, us to believe,
But, we're still not free.

I'm sorry, I'm angry
At economics, politically,
Honest, truthfully, (smile)

I'm sorry, I'm angry,
"Keep them together in poverty"
"Now lets give them guns"
"Now let the drugs flow through"
"Now let us build a penitentiary or two"

I'm sorry, I'm angry,
Our youth are, so damn smart,
They know about guns and drugs,
They know about drugs and guns,

123

They don't know what they're doing,
They don't know they're being done.

I'm sorry, I'm angry
At the Welfare system,
For separating black man,
and black woman,
For if you're there they don't care,
They just stick him and cut you off.

I'm sorry, I'm angry,
At the system, that's fact,
I'm sorry, I'm angry
At a lot of things,
I'm not sorry to be black,

For black is my woman,
For black is my life,
For black is my love,
For black is my stride,
For black is a duration,
For black is pride...

THE FAMILY

The Family, ·
Goes back centuries
Back to days of old.
So, I've been told,
Back in the days,
When as a kid
You know what you did,
And so many others
Seemed to care.

I got to meet
Great Grandma Rose,
All the things
She must've known,
Now the kids of our-- -
Youthfulness have grown,
And it seems
Everyones on their own,
And into their own.

The Family,

A structure

That must remain.

Close and strong

A unit

That must thrive,

And help the babies,

Move on.

The Family,

I remember the times

I shared,

With Grandma Gracie,

With Big Ma and Big Dad,

I recall the times

We had.

The Family,

And it seems like

Only yesterday,

When Grandma would say,

"Sam, leave that boy alone,

He's sorry, he's sorry",

Grandma's were always good,

To get you out of a whipping,
Grandma's were always good.

The Family,
I remember Dad,
(Sam Graham, Jr.)
It seems he held
Us all together,
But, then he was
Taken from me,
I remember Uncle Bob,
and Uncle Jesse,
I loved them, so much
Yet, they to, were
Taken from me,
Why dear God, why?

The Family,
I remember me and Tyrone
And our dog Butch-. -
I remember stories of,
Duke and Dump, and
How they used to thump,

I remember ghost stories

me and my cousins

At Aunt Kay Lee's

I remember hunting frogs

And lizards under

Knocked down trees,

I remember Uncle Kurt,

Uncle Lo, Vernell, Jesse

And Uncle T. (Thurman Graham)

I know all of the above,

Showed great love and

Guided me.

To all my relatives, my Wife and Children,

Aunts, Uncles, Cousins and Families to be,

I love you all, we are all Family

The Family

Lynnor Latham Graham

TO MY MAMA

Thanks to my Mama, for being there,

Thanks to my Mama, who's always cared,

Thanks to my Mama, for being so strong,

Thanks to my Mama, for showing me right from wrong,

Thanks to my Mama, for so much love,

Thanks to my Mama, for her chastising,

Thanks to my Mama, for me realizing

All those sayings, all those deeds,

All those wants, and all those needs,

Thanks to my Mama, for all the little things you do,

Thanks to my Mama, for things,

     I thought, I didn't listen too,

Thanks to my Mama, thanks for being you,

Thanks to my Mama, and Mama, I love you.

     Thanks.....

Lynnor Latham Graham

ABOUT THE AUTHOR

Lynnor L. Latham was born in Boston, MA, a street-wise kid who found his way out of the troubled path of the system he almost fell into. And now as a juvenile youth worker, he cares and tries to steer others away from the direction they are heading in. He is trying to reach as many of those whom are willing to listen and comprehend the love and strength we have as black people.

www.ingramcontent.com/pod-product-compliance
Lightning Source LLC
Chambersburg PA
CBHW020527290526
45786CB00002B/787